Danny Dark

Margaret Johnson

Series Editor: Rob Waring

HEINLE
CENGAGE Learning™

Australia • Brazil • Japan • Korea • Mexico • Singapore • Spain • United Kingdom • United States

HEINLE
CENGAGE Learning™

Page Turners Reading Library
Danny Dark
Margaret Johnson

Publisher: Andrew Robinson

Executive Editor: Sean Bermingham

Senior Development Editor:
Derek Mackrell

Assistant Editors:
Claire Tan, Sarah Tan

Story Editor: Julian Thomlinson

Series Development Editor:
Sue Leather

Director of Global Marketing:
Ian Martin

Content Project Manager:
Tan Jin Hock

Print Buyer:
Susan Spencer

Layout Design and Illustrations:
Redbean Design Pte Ltd

Cover Illustration: Eric Foenander

Photo Credits:
77 Liv Friis-larsen/Shutterstock

ISBN-13: 978-1-4240-1793-5

ISBN-10: 1-4240-1793-9

Heinle
20 Channel Center Street
Boston, Massachusetts 02210
USA

Cengage Learning is a leading provider of customized learning solutions with office locations around the globe, including Singapore, the United Kingdom, Australia, Mexico, Brazil, and Japan. Locate your local office at:
international.cengage.com/region

Cengage Learning products are represented in Canada by Nelson Education, Ltd.

Visit Heinle online at **elt.heinle.com**

Visit our corporate website at
www.cengage.com

Printed in the United States of America
2 3 4 5 6 7 – 14 13 12 11

Contents

Review

Background Reading

People in the story

Sally Clarke
a twenty-nine-year-old
hairdresser and owner of a
hairdressing salon,
The Long and Short

Danny Dark
American manager of the
Richmond Building project

Mr. Morris
owner of the newsagent's
below Sally's salon

Toby
Sally's brother

Julie
Sally's friend

Lily Brookes
employee of
Eastern View TV

The story is set in Norwich, in the UK.

Chapter 1

Electricity

"I guess you'll close The Long and Short when Richmond's opens?"

I was always shocked when I heard people say it and I had heard it every day recently. All my customers asked me. And now Val was asking, too.

The Long and Short is my business: I'm a hairdresser and The Long and Short is my hair salon. Richmond's is the store being built next door. Val Jensen was a good customer of mine, so I didn't show how I felt.

"Why do you say that, Val?" I asked instead, smiling at her in the mirror.

Poor Val, she had no idea I was annoyed with her. Sweet Sally, that's who my customers think I am. If only they knew what I was really thinking about them sometimes! They'd probably think I was Stormy Sally. Or even, on very bad days, Sick Sally.

". . . Why? Because of the new hair and beauty salon that will open in Richmond's, of course," Val said. "People will want to try it, won't they? And the prices will probably be cheaper than yours, as it's a bigger place." She smiled back at me. "The Long and Short is a great little salon. But people like to try out somewhere new, don't they? And they're always looking to save money."

I knew what Val was saying was true, and I was very worried about the future of The Long and Short. But I still felt annoyed. I had worked so hard to make my

business a success. It just wasn't fair that another salon would open up next door.

"They'll soon come back here," I said with more confidence than I felt. "At Richmond's the hairdressers won't have time to talk to them. People like something more personal."

"But by then your business will have failed," Val said. "Believe me, I know. I've seen it all before."

By now I was really angry with her. How could she say that? I felt like "accidentally" cutting too much off one side of Val's hair. Val did know about business, it was true. She had worked in New York and the United Kingdom advising businesses. But I hadn't asked her for her opinion about my situation.

Val still hadn't finished. "No," she went on. "You should sell the business and start a family."

I had to stop cutting Val's hair when she said that. I was too angry to cut her hair safely. "What?" I said, looking her straight in the eye and wondered if I'd heard her correctly.

Val looked at me. She wasn't at all embarrassed. "Find yourself a good man, marry him, and have babies," she said. "Don't leave it until it's too late like I did."

Something in her face made my anger go away. There was real pain in Val's eyes. "Did you want a family?" I asked, but Val didn't answer.

"We aren't talking about me!" she said brightly. "We're talking about you. You're pretty and you're what . . . ? You're almost thirty, but look at yourself and your life! You spend all your time here on your own trying to earn enough money to live . . . What sort of a life is that? I say give it up. See this as an opportunity to start all over and find the really important things in life before it's too late."

I was angry again and this time I couldn't hide it. "Thank you for your advice, Val," I said coldly.

Val laughed. "Thanks, but no thanks, huh?" she said. "Oh well, I tried. It's your life, Sally. You do what you want."

"I will," I told her coldly, and after that we didn't speak again until I finished cutting her hair.

When Val got up to leave, she smiled at me. "Sorry if I made you mad," she said. "I like you, that's all. I don't want to see your business fail. And I don't want to see you get hurt."

"Don't worry," I said. "I can look after myself."

Val smiled. "OK then. Good-bye, Sally."

"Good-bye, Val."

As the door closed behind her, I wanted to scream. Or just throw things around. But I had another customer coming soon, so I did neither of those things. Instead, I took a deep breath and put on some makeup. Putting on makeup almost always makes me feel better. But that morning, I couldn't stop thinking about what Val had said. I was really worried about what was going to happen to my business. If people stopped coming to the salon, I could survive okay for about six months. I had some money in the bank, but it was money I wanted to use to buy a house. I really wanted my own house, and I didn't want to spend that money.

I was just finishing my makeup when I heard someone coming up the stairs to the salon. After a few moments, the door opened. "I'll be right with you," I called.

"That's OK," said a deep man's voice. An American man's voice. Had the salon somehow been moved to New York without me realizing it? I turned round quickly, a smile on my face . . . and saw one of the most attractive men I had ever seen—a tall, slim man with black hair and green eyes.

"Oh!" I said, and the man smiled.

"You were expecting me, I hope?" he asked. "The name's Dark. Danny Dark."

My face was red, and I suddenly felt like a stupid teenager. "Of course," I said. "Take a seat." I pulled a chair out for him. "I'll . . . I'll just get you something to wear over your clothes. An overall. I'll get you an overall."

He smiled. "Thanks."

I could feel myself going hot just looking at his smile. I quickly went next door and waved my hand up and down in front of my face to cool it down. What was wrong with me? I was twenty-nine, not twelve! Okay, so the man was attractive, but this was just stupid.

Taking a few deep breaths and putting a smile on my face, I went back into the salon.

"OK," I said brightly. "What can I do for you today?"

"I'd like my hair washed and cut, please," the man said. What was his name? Danny. Danny Dark. That was it. "OK," I said, still in the same bright voice. I looked at him in the mirror. He was smiling at me. "Oh," I said, embarrassed. "I forgot to get you an overall, didn't I?"

"You did," he said, his smile getting bigger and bigger.

My face was going red again. "I'll just go and umm . . . get one," I said.

Neither of us spoke while I washed his hair.

Usually, I don't think about it. I just get on with washing a customer's hair while we talk about the weather or what we're doing that weekend—something like that. But this time it was different. I couldn't think of anything to say, not a thing. My fingers somehow seemed to be able to feel more than usual. Oh, I can't really explain it properly. You'll just have to believe me. It was as if my fingers on Danny Dark's head were making electricity. Like they were on fire.

"It's quiet in here today." When he spoke, I jumped with surprise.

"No," I said. "I mean, I've got customers all day."

By now I was drying his hair with a towel. He smiled at me in the mirror. "I see," he said. "You just have one customer in at a time?"

I put the towel down and started to comb his hair. "Yes," I said. "It's my own business and I work alone. It would be too expensive to pay someone else to work here. You have to think very hard about everything when you run a business. Of course, I've worked with other people before . . ."

He was smiling at me in the mirror again.

"Sorry," I said, and laughed. "I'm talking too much, aren't I?"

"Not at all," he said, but I knew he was just being nice.

"What brings you to England?" I asked, and his smile disappeared.

"A relationship," he said.

People often tell hairdressers private information about their lives. Danny Dark seemed to be no different. I just said "Oh?" and waited, and he soon carried on talking.

"Yes. She lived here in the UK, here in Norwich, in fact. I lived in New York, we were flying backwards and forwards to meet, and . . . well, it was difficult. Not getting anywhere very much . . . Anyway, by the time I realized she wasn't the person I wanted to stay with forever, you know, The One, I had an apartment—I mean a flat—and a job. Take my advice, Miss . . . ?" He looked at me.

"Sally," I told him.

"Take my advice, Sally; never move to a foreign country because of a relationship."

From the way he said it, I knew he expected me to laugh, and I did. I felt like laughing actually, because now I knew he was single. Handsome, funny, and single—it was too good to be true.

"What is your job, Mr. Dark?" I asked, and then he laughed.

"Please," he said, "call me Danny. Mr. Dark makes me sound like someone in a frightening movie."

"A vampire movie?" I asked, laughing.

"Something like that," Danny smiled.

"No," I said, "you haven't got the right teeth to be a vampire."

Danny Dark smiled, showing me his perfect white teeth. "I'm quite pleased about that," he said.

We talked on, I can't remember what about exactly. I was just so pleased we were talking easily to each other I didn't stop to think if Danny had mentioned his job. I didn't really get a chance to think about it. I was too busy cutting his hair, and anyway Danny started asking me questions about myself.

"So, how long have you been a hairdresser?" "How long has The Long and Short been open?" "Do you like hairdressing?" "Have you ever thought about doing something else?" Looking back now, I can see that Danny asked me question after question about hairdressing and my salon, The Long and Short. At the time, I just thought he was interested in me; I thought he was asking me lots of questions because he wanted to get to know me better. I even thought he might ask me out on a date. I wanted him to ask me out on a date.

Danny's haircut was almost finished. Ask me, I thought. Ask me out.

But he didn't ask me out. Instead he looked at me in the mirror and asked, "Are you worried about the future with the building going up next door?"

I was so tired of being asked about Richmond's. And now Danny was asking me. And he hadn't asked me out! "Yes," I said. "Of course I am. But worrying doesn't help much, does it?"

"What are you going to do?" he asked.

His haircut was finished. I picked up a hand mirror to show him the back. "I'm not sure," I said. "But I do know one thing; I'll never give up because of Richmond's. Not even if they offered money for me to close. Never."

Danny Dark didn't seem to be interested in his haircut. He turned away from the mirror to look me right in the eye, his face absolutely serious. "Are you sure you'd never sell The Long and Short? Not even for three hundred thousand pounds?" he asked.

Chapter 2

Bad news

I looked at him, shocked. "What?"

Danny stood up and held out his hand. "Let me introduce myself properly; I'm Danny Dark, manager of the Richmond Building Project." He was still wearing the hairdressing overall. It was made of green material with small flowers all over it because all the black ones were in the wash. At any other time I might have thought it was funny that such an important, manly man was wearing a woman's overall. But just then I was too angry to think it was funny.

"And as manager of the project, I'm in a position to offer you three hundred thousand pounds for your salon. Of course, Richmond's wouldn't keep it as it is; the store will have its own salon, as I'm sure you know. No, we'd pull down the salon and build an extra car park on this land for busy times."

My face was bright red. I was so angry I felt as if the top of my head might blow off. I had thought this man liked me. I had thought he was going to ask me out. And all the time he was here to offer me money so he could destroy The Long and Short—just to build a car park!

"Get out," I said.

Danny Dark smiled at me, reaching behind him to try to take the overall off. "Come on, Sally," he said in a voice that made me want to throw a hairdryer at his head.

"Don't be like that. I like you. You're a nice woman. I'd hate to think of The Long and Short failing when Richmond's salon opens. You must see that this is a good deal for you."

"Get out," I said again.

Danny held up his hands. "OK. OK, I'm on my way. But please, Sally, think about it."

I opened my mouth to speak, but Danny got there first. "OK," he said. "I know; get out. Don't worry; I'm going. But perhaps you could take this overall off for me first? I can't do it."

For the first time since he had made his offer, I smiled. "Can't you?" I said. "Oh, well, don't worry. It really suits you."

Danny was still smiling. "I'll be in touch again, Sally," he said, and walked to the door, still wearing the overall.

I listened to him as he went down the stairs. I went to the window to watch him walk away. Two teenagers were passing by, and they looked at him in the overall. I was very pleased when they laughed at him, and I laughed too, waiting for Danny to get angry. But he didn't get angry. He just laughed and pointed up toward the salon. It was easy to imagine him saying, "This is the latest thing to wear. If you want one, you can get one in there!" And suddenly I felt so angry I wanted to run down and shout something unpleasant at him.

But before I could, he walked around the corner out of sight. It was only then that I remembered he hadn't paid me for his haircut.

"Can you believe it?" I said to my friend Julie over coffee. "Because I can't! I keep remembering how I smiled at him, listening to his every word like some silly teenager. And all the time he was just there to try and buy me out! It makes me feel ill, it really does."

I'd been so angry, I closed the salon for lunch. I absolutely had to tell somebody about it all. The person I needed to

speak to most of all was Mr. Morris, who owned the newsagent's below the salon. If Danny Dark wanted to buy The Long and Short, then he must have made an offer to Mr. Morris as well. But when I went into the newspaper shop, Mr. Morris was out. So I called my friend Julie instead.

"It wasn't even a good offer either," Julie said kindly. "The Long and Short is worth more than that."

"It is," I agreed. "Not that I want to sell anyway."

"Of course you don't," said Julie.

"I've put so much work into that place."

"Of course you have," said Julie.

I've known Julie since college. At times like this, friends like Julie are just what you need. "Thanks, Julie," I said.

Julie smiled at me over her cup of coffee. We were in one of our favorite Norwich cafés next to the market in the city center. It's a good place to watch the world go by, but today I wouldn't have noticed if the Queen of England walked by.

"Thanks for what?" Julie asked.

"Listening."

"That's OK," Julie said. "I was having a very boring morning." Julie is a beautician, but at the moment she's working in an office because it was the only job she could get. She hates it.

"I wish my morning had been boring," I said, looking unhappily out of the window.

"So, you say you liked him, this Danny Dark?" Julie asked. "Before you discovered who he was, I mean?"

For a moment I remembered that feeling of electricity when I'd been washing his hair. "Yes," I said, "I did. But that's not

important, is it? I do know who he is now, don't I? A dirty spy. A bad guy."

"Mmm," said Julie with a smile. "That's just the type of man I like best."

Once again I remembered that electricity, but then I shook my head. "Julie," I said, "you're sick!"

Julie laughed. "True," she said. "I'm sorry he turned out to be no good though. It's a long time since you've felt like that about a man."

It was true. My last serious relationship had ended three years before, and since then I hadn't met anyone I really wanted to go out with.

"Believe me," I said, "even if he didn't want to destroy The Long and Short, Danny Dark isn't good boyfriend material. He's dangerous—the type to break four women's hearts before breakfast."

Once again, Julie laughed. "When can I meet him?" she joked.

I felt better as I walked back to the salon. Julie always manages to make me laugh, and laughing always makes me feel better.

"Hi there, Sally," a man's voice called to me, and I looked over.

It was Sam, the man who managed the builders working on the Richmond building. I'd met him about two months before, and liked him right away. He was a large man with lots of wild blond hair, and he always had a big smile for me.

"I hear you met the boss?" he said and laughed at the face I made.

"Yes," I said, "I met him. And I'm not in a hurry to meet him again."

"He made you an offer for the salon, didn't he?"

"Yes," I told him. "A very low offer. A silly offer."

"Which you refused?"

"I certainly did! I'm not stupid."

Sam looked a bit worried. "Well," he said, "just be careful, won't you? Mr. Dark doesn't give up easily. When he decides he wants something, he usually gets it."

I walked on toward the salon. "Don't worry about me, Sam," I said over my shoulder. "The Danny Darks of this world don't worry me. The Long and Short is not for sale. End of story."

It was a busy afternoon with one customer after another. There wasn't even time to have a cup of coffee. By five o'clock, my meeting with Danny Dark seemed like . . . well, if not exactly a dream, then not quite real. Had I imagined the strong feelings I'd had for the man? All that stuff about electricity! How could I feel like that one moment and then hate him the next moment? It was silly.

But then the salon door opened, Danny Dark walked in, and it happened all over again.

"Sally," he said in a voice like dark chocolate, and that was all it took. My face went red, my hands shook—the electricity was back.

But there was no way I was going to show how I felt so I turned away from him, hiding my face. "You aren't welcome here," I told him coldly. "I'd like you to go, please."

He smiled again. "Well, that's a little more friendly than 'get out,'" he said. "Come on, Sally, you don't have to hate me. This is just business. I've already told you I like you. In fact, if it weren't for the car park thing, I'd ask you out on a date."

My heart jumped a little, but I carefully didn't let Danny see it. "Don't even try it," I said turning to face him.

He smiled. "Well," he said, "maybe not today." Then he took an envelope from his pocket and held it out to me. "This is the money for the haircut," he said.

I took the envelope from him. Business was business, after all. "Thank you."

"You did a good job," he said, looking at himself in the mirror.

I was standing by the window, and down in the street below I could see a parking attendant writing a ticket for an expensive car parked in a No Parking area. I hoped it was Danny's car.

"Oh," he said as he turned to the door, "there's a little extra in there for the overall. I had to cut it to get it off."

"Right," I said.

"And there's a letter in there as well. I thought I'd put Richmond's offer for The Long and Short in writing." And then, before I could tell him what he could do with his letter, he walked to the door.

"See you soon," he said, and then he was gone.

"Oh!" I said. Feeling angry all over again, I quickly opened the letter, carefully taking the money out before putting the letter in the rubbish.

When I looked out of the window again, I saw Danny talking to the parking attendant. So, it was his car. Great! Something good was going to happen today then! But as I watched, Danny smiled that smile of his, and I realized that the parking attendant was a woman. Within seconds Danny was getting in his car, and the attendant was walking away with a smile on her face.

I wanted to scream very loudly.

I was just getting ready to go home when the shop door opened again. I turned quickly, half thinking it would be Danny again, but instead it was Mr. Morris who owned the newsagent's below.

"Hello, Sally," he said, and I could tell immediately from his face why he'd come.

"You've had a letter from Richmond's too, haven't you?" I said.

"Yes, I have," Mr. Morris said. "They've made me an offer for the shop."

"Me, too," I told him. "Oh, it makes me so angry! Who do they think they are, coming here and trying to shut down our businesses?"

Mr. Morris looked uncomfortable. "You see, the thing is," he began, and once again, I knew what he was going to say.

"Oh no," I said. "You're thinking of accepting their offer, aren't you?"

Mr. Morris didn't seem to want to look at me. "Yes, I am," he said.

This was truly the worst day of my life. "But you can't do that!" I told him. "Please. Look, let's talk about this. Come for a drink with me."

"Well, I don't know," said Mr. Morris unhappily.

"Please," I said again, and I took hold of his arm, really wanting to make him agree. He couldn't sell out. He couldn't. His shop was below mine; with him gone it would be very hard for me to fight to stay open. Besides, we shared the expense of maintaining the building; it would be a lot of money for me to find on my own. And it wouldn't be long before the building needed some work.

Mr. Morris obviously felt sorry for me. "OK," he said finally, "but I can't stay long."

So I locked up the shop, and we went for a drink at the pub the Queen's Head on the corner of the road. "Listen, we can't let them win," I told him when we were sitting down at a table. "It's just not fair. We were here first. Richmond's thinks they can treat us badly just because they're bigger than us. It's happening all the time these days with big companies. Small businesses are closing down everywhere because of companies like Richmond's. Somebody has to stand and fight."

"You're young, it's different for you," Mr. Morris said. "But I'm too old to fight, Sally."

"But you've put so much into your business," I told him. "How long have you been there? Twenty years?"

"Twenty-five," Mr. Morris said sadly.

"Twenty-five years!" I repeated. "You can't throw all of that away. Anyway, I thought you wanted to give the business to your son when you reached sixty-five."

"I will," Mr. Morris said, but from the sound of his voice, I could tell he'd already given up. "But I don't want to give him a bad business, do I? Richmond's will sell newspapers and magazines on the ground floor of the store. There isn't enough business for two newsagent's on one street."

I couldn't think of anything else to say. "Well look," I said, "don't do anything about it yet, please." If I had time to think, then maybe I could come up with some plan. I had absolutely no idea what, but there must be something I could do. I couldn't, wouldn't let Richmond's and Danny Dark win.

I guess it must have been obvious to Mr. Morris how badly

I wanted to keep my business open. "Well," he said, "the letter said I had two weeks to think about their offer, so I suppose I can wait until then."

I was really pleased. "Oh, thank you!" I said.

But Mr. Morris shook his head. "But I don't think it will make any difference, Sally," he warned me.

Just then the pub door opened, and Danny Dark walked in. I looked angrily in his direction. "There he is," I said to Mr. Morris. "The man behind all this trouble."

"He's just doing his job," Mr. Morris said. "I thought he was a nice man actually, even if I didn't like what he had to say."

I was about to tell Mr. Morris he was wrong when Danny saw us and came over.

"Why hello, Sally, Ivan," he said.

Ivan. I'd worked in the same building as Mr. Morris for almost five years, and never found out his name was Ivan! He'd always just been Mr. Morris to me. But Danny "full-of-friendly-smiles" Dark had found out his name in five minutes.

"Can I buy you a drink?" Danny asked.

Before Mr. Morris could think of accepting, I stood up. "We were just leaving," I told him coolly, and Danny smiled.

"Another time then," he said. "Have a good evening both of you." And he left.

I looked at Mr. Morris. "Two weeks," I said. "Give me two weeks. I'll think of something; I promise I will."

Chapter 3

Toby's story

It started to rain as I walked home. By the time I reached my flat, I was very wet. It was supposed to be summer, but so far we had seen very little sunshine in Norwich. Still, rain suited my mood, I supposed.

Deciding I needed to warm up, I took my clothes off and stood under the shower. The next moment I was screaming. The water was very cold—like ice, in fact. I must have forgotten to put the water heater on before I left for work. Quickly drying myself with a towel, I put my clothes back on and went into the living room to watch TV while I waited for the water to heat up. But when I tried to put the TV on, it didn't work.

"Oh, I don't believe it!" I said to the empty room. I knew exactly what was wrong; I have to put coins in a meter box to pay for electricity as I use it in this flat. The meter must need more money. I went to look for some coins, but I didn't have any.

"Oh no!" I was going to have to go out again to get some.

Walking back out into the rain, I thought how bad it was living in a flat that wasn't mine. True, I had painted the walls nice sunny colors, but the table, chairs, and other things in the flat were old and made of dark wood. I couldn't paint that. But the flat was cheap, and that was why I stayed there for now. I got a take-out meal while I was out because it was getting late and I was hungry. I took the food and the coins for the electricity meter back to the flat. As I walked in, the phone was ringing, and I hurried to answer it.

"Hello?"

"Hi, Sally," said a bright voice on the other end of the line. "Have I called at a bad time?" It was my brother, Toby, who works for a newspaper.

Suddenly forgetting all about being hungry and wet, I sat down on the sofa with a smile. I'd just had a great idea. "No, Toby," I said, "you haven't called at a bad time at all. In fact, you couldn't have called at a better time." And then I quickly told him the whole story about Richmond's, Danny Dark, and my fight to stay in business.

Two days later, I hurried downstairs during my lunch break to buy a newspaper. Toby had promised something about my situation would appear in the paper today, and I couldn't wait to see it. Quickly paying for the paper, I began to open it, and then realized I didn't have to. The story was on the front page!

"Big Boots, No Heart!" That was the title of Toby's story. Smiling, I quickly read on. "A city with no small shops or businesses; that's what Norwich will become if the people behind the new Richmond's store do what they want to do."

I read on. "A hairdressing salon and a newsagent's will have to close when Richmond's destroys them to build an unnecessary car park. Sally Clarke, 29, the owner of The Long and Short hair salon, said yesterday, 'I've built The Long and Short up from nothing. It's successful now, but Richmond's only offered me a very small amount of money for it. I think they thought I would be pleased with that, but I'm not. Why should I have to close just because Richmond's decides to come to town?'"

"Good work, Toby," I said to myself. "Good work!" I looked at the girl serving in the newsagent's. "Where's Mr. Morris?" I asked.

"He's out this morning," she said.

"Well, tell him to look at this when he gets back!" I said, waving the newspaper at her. Then I hurried back to the salon to phone my brother.

But I hadn't managed to get through to Toby on the phone before I heard the salon door open behind me.

"I'll be right with you," I said, but when I looked round there was Danny Dark, and he was holding a newspaper. Deciding my call to my brother could wait, I put the phone down and smiled at him. I was feeling good, I admit it. I felt as if I had really got back at Danny and Richmond's through Toby's story.

Without saying anything to me, Danny sat himself down in one of my chairs and looked down at the newspaper. "This makes Richmond's out to be a really bad company that wants to change the way Norwich looks forever."

"Well, aren't you?" I said.

"No, Sally, we are not." Danny smiled at me as if I were a child. "We simply need to build a car park."

"Well, you're not building it here!" I told him angrily.

Danny was still smiling. "You look even more beautiful when you're angry," he told me.

"That's like a line from an old movie," I told him angrily.

Danny smiled. "Maybe," he said. "But it's still true. Come on, Sally, forget about all of this and come out on a date with me. You know you want to."

It was the second time he'd mentioned going out on a date. Did he really mean it? Or did he just want me to say yes so he could try to get me to change my mind about selling the salon? Not that I was going to say yes, of course. "Even if I did want to go out with you, which I don't," I said, "how could I possibly forget all about this? This is my business, the business I built up from nothing."

Danny put the newspaper under his arm and got to his feet. "So that's a no then?" he said.

I felt like throwing something at him. "Get out!" I said.

Danny didn't move. "Look, Sally," he said more seriously, "I know this is hard for you. And I'm sorry that Richmond's plans are bad news for you. But I'm just doing my job, that's all."

I picked up a hairbrush, thinking about throwing it at him. I'm sure he could see what I was thinking. Anyway, he walked quickly to the door.

"OK," he said, "I'm going. See you soon, I hope."

Chapter 4

Sunday meeting

It was the following Sunday when I saw him next. One of the good things about my flat is where it is; it's in the north of Norwich near a lovely place called Mousehold Heath. Mousehold Heath has lots of trees and grass, and people go there with their families or to walk their dogs. It's almost like being in the country, even though you're still in the city. Anyway, I go running there as often as I can; it keeps me healthy and it helps me to think. And that Sunday, after a terrible week, I had a lot to think about.

The ground can get very muddy on the Heath after a lot of rain. I don't mind getting dirty; I just wear my old clothes and have a nice shower when I get home. That Sunday as I went on my run, I was so busy trying to think what I could do to save the salon, I didn't even notice the dirt. The newspaper story had been good; lots of my customers had seen it and talked to me about it. But now I needed something bigger—something that would get everybody talking.

But what?

As I came round a corner, I was deep in thought. I didn't see Danny at first. But then I heard a young American voice and looked up.

"Uncle Daniel, there's mud all over your pants!"

"That's because you two are running too close to me!" I recognized Danny's voice and immediately stopped running. Moving quickly to stand behind a large tree, I stood and watched. Danny was with two children—a girl and a boy. They were about twenty meters ahead, walking in the same direction as I. They all had their backs to me, so I was able to watch them for a long time.

It was very enjoyable. This was not the Danny I had seen in my salon. That Danny had been confident and at home, dressed in a business suit. This Danny was dressed in dirty jeans and was walking very slowly, looking down at the ground all the time. He didn't look confident at all away from his work.

"Which way do we go now, Uncle Daniel?" asked the boy, and Danny stopped to look around.

"I don't know," he said.

"Are we lost, Uncle Daniel?" asked the girl.

"No!" Danny replied angrily. "We aren't lost."

"So, which way is it then?" asked the boy.

"If you'd only keep quiet for a minute, I might be able to think!"

Danny sounded so angry, I wanted to laugh.

"Well, I think it's this way," the boy said, pulling at Danny's arm.

"No, it's this way," said the girl, pulling at his other arm.

"Stop pulling at me, both of you!" Danny shouted, but it was too late. As I watched, he fell over, right in the worst of the mud.

It was so funny I just had to laugh. Loudly. Danny looked in my direction. So did the girl and boy.

"Uncle Danny," said the girl, "that tree's laughing at us."

"It's not the tree, stupid," said the boy. "Somebody's hiding behind it!"

I had no choice then; I had to come out.

"It's a lady," said the girl as I began to walk toward them, still laughing.

"Sally!" said Danny.

"Do you know her?" asked the boy.

"Yes," said Daniel, still sounding annoyed. "I do."

By the time I reached them, Danny was up on his feet again, his blue jeans black with dirt.

"Oh dear," I said with a smile.

"OK," said Danny angrily.

"You're very dirty, Uncle Daniel," said the girl, looking at his jeans.

"And we're lost," said the boy. "I didn't want to come for a walk anyway!"

"Me neither!" said the girl.

"OK, children, thank you," said Danny. "That's enough. This is Sally Clarke. Sally, these are my sister's children, Brian and Susan. They're over here for a visit."

"Hi there," I said, still smiling at the memory of Danny Dark lying in the mud.

"Do you know how to get out of this place?" Brian asked me.

"Yes, I do," I said. "I live near here."

"Uncle Daniel doesn't," said Susan. "We came in his car."

"Which car park are you parked in?" I asked Danny, and he looked unhappy.

"You mean there's more than one?" he asked.

I smiled again. "There are three."

"There was a little sign for a golf course," Brian told me helpfully.

"The golf course?" I said. "I know it."

"Only Uncle Daniel wouldn't let us go on it," Susan said. Clearly it had not been a very successful afternoon out.

"You wouldn't have enjoyed it," Daniel said.

"We're not enjoying this!" Brian told him.

Danny looked at me. He obviously found being an uncle difficult, and I almost felt sorry for him. "Can you tell me which way we have to walk, Sally? Please?" he asked.

I looked back at him. If the children hadn't been there, I might have given him the wrong directions to get him lost. I couldn't think of one reason why I should help him. But the children were there.

"You need to turn around and walk back in that direction," I said. "Then when you get to the big tree, turn right, then go straight, along between some tall trees."

Danny was looking doubtful. "Did you say left by the big tree?" he asked, and I shook my head.

"No, right. Look, would you like me to take you?"

He smiled at me in the same way he had smiled at the parking attendant. "If you wouldn't mind, Sally, that would be really kind of you. I know Brian and Susan will be ready for their lunch soon."

But actually, once we were on the way back to their car, Brian and Susan seemed to get some extra energy from somewhere. When they ran off in front, leaving Danny and me on our own, I wanted to call them back. The last thing I wanted was to be alone with Danny.

The silence between us grew. This was not what I had expected when I had set off for my run, and I just couldn't think of anything—not one thing—to say. It was that electricity again.

Finally, Danny spoke. "So, do you come here often?" he asked, and when I looked at him, he was smiling. "Sorry, that was like something someone would say in a bar or pub," he said.

"A pick-up line?" I asked and immediately wished I hadn't. Even with mud all over his pants, Danny was a very attractive man. If we had met in a bar, and he had tried to "pick me up," then things might have been very different.

"Something like that," Danny said, still smiling.

There was a bird singing in a tree close to us, and I looked up at it so that I could look away from Danny's smile. It was a dangerous smile; it made me feel soft and weak, and I shouldn't feel soft and weak around Danny. It wasn't a good idea.

"What is that bird?" he asked, looking up at the tree with me.

"It's a robin. See, it's red at the front." Danny's head was very close to mine as we watched the bird. Too close.

"So it is," Danny said, and then he laughed. "You know, the first time I saw one of your robins, I couldn't believe how small they were. American robins are much bigger."

The robin flew away, and I walked on. "In answer to your question," I said, "I do come here quite often. I find it very relaxing."

"It's certainly very beautiful."

"Except for the mud?" I said, and he laughed.

"Yes," he agreed. "Except for the mud."

I looked at him. "Are you one of those people who always keeps their flat looking like a picture in a magazine?" I asked.

Brian and Susan had come back without me noticing. "He sure is!" Brian said.

"We have to take our shoes off in the hall!" Susan said.

"And he doesn't let us eat pizza in front of the TV, until he's put a cover on the sofa," Brian complained.

"The sofa is white," Danny explained, shaking his head.

I smiled at him. "If I had a white sofa, it wouldn't stay white for long," I said.

"Yeah," Danny said, "that doesn't surprise me." He was laughing at me, but somehow I didn't feel annoyed. For the moment anyway we were getting on well. I was joking with him, and he was joking with me. It was fun.

But then Brian asked, "How do you know Uncle Daniel, Sally?" and everything changed. I remembered it all: The Long and Short, Danny's offer, the extra car park, everything. How could I have let myself forget for one second?

"It's a long story," I told Brian, and when I looked at Daniel again, my face was cold.

"The car park's just ahead through the trees," I told him. "You can't miss it. Bye, Brian, bye, Susan; it was nice to meet you."

"Oh," said Danny, "are you going? I was going to invite you back for a cup of coffee."

Just for a moment I looked at him. He had sounded as if he really wanted me to go. And if things had been different, I would have loved to go—have a cup of coffee, see what Danny's flat was like, and spend some more time with the children. The kind of things you might do when you want to get to know somebody better.

But things weren't different. Danny was still the man who wanted to close down my business.

"No thanks," I said. "I've got plans today." And then I turned and ran back through the trees toward home.

Chapter 5

The big haircut

"There's been a lot of interest in the story. If you are going to follow it up, you need to do something while people still remember it."

Toby, Julie, and I were having a drink together in a pub in the city center after work. I'd asked them both to meet me because I wanted their advice. It had been great to see the story about The Long and Short in the newspaper, but I wasn't sure what to do next. I thought they might be able to help me think of something.

It was a nice evening for once, so we were sitting at a table outside.

"You're right, Toby," Julie said. "But what?"

"I don't know," he said. "But it needs to be something big; something that will get one of the television companies interested."

I had been busy thinking, and suddenly I put my drink down with a smile. "I think I've got it," I said and turned toward Julie. "Have you still got the addresses of everybody who was in our hairdressing course?"

"Yes," she said. "I think so. Why? We finished our hairdressing course years ago."

"Because we're going to need their help," I said. "And we're also going to need chairs, a lot of them."

"Chairs?" By now, both Toby and Julie were looking at me as if I were crazy.

"The school!" I said. "We can get some chairs from the school hall down the road. Mr. Morris's brother looks after the building; he's the caretaker."

"Sally," said Toby, "what do you need chairs for?"

"Yes," said Julie, "tell us your plan!"

So, still with a great big smile on my face, I did.

It took a lot of phone calls and hard work, but between us we managed to get everything ready in three days. On the big day, Julie took some time off work, and I closed The Long and Short for the afternoon. Toby had phoned some of the people he knew at one of the television companies, and they had promised to come along during the afternoon. And now, at exactly two o'clock in the afternoon, we were ready to start.

In front of the Richmond Building there was a long line of hairdressers and customers. The hairdressers were people Julie and I knew from our course and students who were doing the course now. There were about thirty of us in all. The customers were their friends and family. They were all wearing overalls and sitting in the chairs Mr. Morris's brother had gotten for us from the school hall. The hairdressers were all standing behind them, ready to start cutting hair. It was going to be the largest number of haircuts to be done at the same time, or at least, the largest number to have been done at the same time in Norwich.

"Thank you for coming here today, everybody!" I shouted, and I had to shout really loudly to be heard over the noise of the cars on the street. "OK, everyone: five, four, three, two, one, start cutting!"

Hurrying over to my own place behind my customer, I got to work myself. My customer was someone who came to the salon every month, and she had jumped at the chance when I'd asked her if she could come along.

"This is amazing, Sally," she said now. "I'm so happy to be a part of it."

I smiled at her as I brushed her hair. "It's very good of you to help," I told her.

"No problem," she said. "A free haircut and a chance to be on TV! How could I refuse?"

The lights changed farther up the road, and, just for a moment, the cars stopped coming past. The only noises I could hear were the sounds of excited talking and busy scissors. And all at once I felt really happy. I had achieved all this—me, Sally Clarke. These hairdressers were all here today because I had spoken to them. Not only about what was happening to me, but also about how things might be for them one day. We were all here because we believed we had to stop large companies from walking all over small businesses. I hoped there would be so many stories about this event on television and in newspapers that Richmond's would be forced to change their mind about the car park.

The light changed to green, and the cars began to come past again. Some drivers slowed down to see what was happening. One man shouted to us out of his car window, "Can you give me a wash and cut?"

We all laughed. "Of course!" I shouted back. "And bring your friends!" It was a long time since I'd had so much fun.

Then Julie called to me, "Sally, it's the TV company!"

And when I looked, I saw that she was right. A television lorry was just parking across the road. Great! As I watched, two men and a woman got out. The men opened the back of the lorry and started to get a camera out. The woman, who was dressed in a suit, came over to us.

"I'm Lily Brookes from Eastern View TV," she said to one of the girls. "Who's the person to speak to about all this?"

"You want to speak to Sally, over there," the girl told her, and the next moment Lily Brookes was walking in my direction.

My customer laughed. "This is it," she said, "our chance to be on TV!"

Lily Brookes stopped in front of me. "Sally?" she asked and smiled.

"Yes," I said, "I'm Sally."

Lily held out her hand to me. I shook it. "Lily Brookes from Eastern View TV. We'd like to interview you for tonight's show, if that's OK with you?"

"That would be amazing!" I said, sounding like a schoolgirl, and Lily smiled.

"All right," she said. "That's great. We'll just get the rest of the stuff out of the lorry, and then we'll make a start."

I was still smiling. "OK."

As Lily turned away, I picked up a hairbrush and quickly used it on my own hair. After all, I wanted to look good for the cameras, didn't I?

Lily soon returned with the cameraman. "OK, Sally," she said in a friendly voice, "perhaps you could just tell us what's happening today and why you decided to do this."

And so I did. I told her about the car park, Danny's offer, about phoning up all the hairdressers and getting the chairs from the school hall; everything. Then I introduced her to many of the other hairdressers.

"Do you think this will work, Sally?" Lily asked me after a while. "Do you think you can stop Richmond's from closing your salon?"

And suddenly I remembered what the whole thing was about. Today had been a lot of fun. Being interviewed for TV had been fun. But I was here because I wanted to save The Long and Short. The Long and Short would never survive if a new hair and beauty salon at Richmond's opened.

For the first time since Lily Brookes had gotten out of the TV lorry, I stopped smiling. "This has to work," I told her seriously. "It just has to."

Lily was nodding her head at me kindly. I knew she was just going to thank me for my time and end the interview. But before she could, several things happened at the same time. It began to rain. It rained hard. Then a very large lorry stopped in front of the Richmond building. It was so big that cars couldn't get past it. And Sam came to look for me.

"Hi, Sally," he said. "Sorry, but we need to get that lorry in, and some of you are in the way. Could you ask people to move for just a moment to let the driver get past you?"

Sam was as nice as ever, and he had asked me nicely. I felt badly about not doing what he asked. But I took a look at Lily's face and I knew exactly what was going on in her head. She was thinking that the story might be about to get more exciting.

"I'm really sorry, Sam," I said. "But I can't ask them to move."

Sam looked as if he couldn't quite believe it. "But the cars can't get past," he told me. "The whole city will soon come to a stop if we're not careful. We'll all be in big trouble."

I felt bad about that, too, but I had to think about myself. I hadn't started all of this. I just wanted to run my business, that was all. "And I'll be in big trouble if Richmond's make me close The Long and Short," I told him.

Sam looked unhappy. "I know that," he said, "and I'm really sorry for you. But look, I'm going to have to tell Mr. Dark about this, Sally."

But Sam didn't need to tell Danny, because, behind Sam, I could see him walking through the rain toward us. And he wasn't looking at all happy.

He stopped in front of us. He was wearing a business suit with no coat, and he looked completely wet. "This all looks like a lot of fun, Sally," he said. "But if you could just move to let the lorry through? I'm sure Sam has already asked you very nicely."

The cameraman was busy. I looked straight into Danny's eyes. Somehow with all these friends around me, I didn't feel afraid of him the way I usually did.

"Has Richmond's decided not to build an extra car park on my land?" I asked him.

Danny looked annoyed. "No," he said. "Of course they haven't."

"Well," I said, "then I can't ask people to move, I'm afraid."

Lily stepped forward. "Sir?" she said to Danny. "Can you tell us why you think a car park is more important than a person's business?"

I felt a jump of excitement inside me at Lily's words. She was on my side!

Danny didn't answer Lily's question. He didn't even look in her direction. "I don't think you understand, Sally," he said to me. "Every hour these men can't work costs Richmond's thousands. I could lose my job over something like this."

I shook my head. "You could lose your job? What about me if the salon closes? Call the police if you want to; we aren't going anywhere!"

But in the end Danny didn't need to call the police, because just at that moment, a police car stopped next to the TV lorry. Soon a very large policeman was getting out of the car and walking toward us.

That was the end of it really. Nobody wanted to be taken away by the police. Besides, the haircuts were all finished and the customers—and the hairdressers—were all getting very wet. And it didn't matter anyway. We'd already achieved what we wanted to achieve. Tonight thousands of people would see us on TV.

"Would you mind if we got The Long and Short on film?" Lily asked me after I'd thanked everybody for coming. "It would add a bit to the story."

"Of course not," I told her, and off we went.

"This is lovely," Lily told me after she'd had a good look around. "It would be terrible if you had to close." Suddenly, I felt like crying, but Lily didn't notice. She was looking at herself in the mirror. "Oh no," she said, touching her wet hair. "I've got a date tonight, and I haven't got time to go home first either."

I put a bright smile on my face. "Take a seat," I said. "I'll do your hair for you."

Lily smiled. "That's kind of you. Thank you very much," she said.

In the end, I did more for Lily than just cutting and drying her hair. Her clothes were wet, so, as we were about the same size, I said she could change into one of my dresses. I always keep some clothes in the salon for times when I'm going out right after work, and I thought one of my dresses would look really good on Lily.

Lily looked at it doubtfully at first. "I'm not sure red is really good for me," she said, but I knew it would look great on her.

"I think it is," I said. "Try it on."

So she did, and when I gave her a belt and a soft scarf to wear with it, she was very pleased with the results. "I look really good," she said with surprise, looking at herself in the mirror.

"With your color hair, strong colors suit you," I told her. "You should wear them more often."

"From now on I will," said Lily with a smile, putting on her coat. "Now, I'd better go. Don't forget to watch TV tonight, and good luck with your fight."

I was almost afraid to watch myself on television, but Julie came home with me to my flat, and then Toby arrived with a pizza and some wine, so it turned into a bit of a party.

"Listen to you!" Toby joked when my interview with Lily was being shown. "You'll be leading the country soon!"

I gave Toby's arm a friendly push, but really I was pleased. The Sally Clarke speaking on the television sounded confident and knowledgeable, even when Danny appeared.

"This all looks like a lot of fun, Sally," I listened to him say. "But could you just move to let the lorry through?"

"He could have shouted at me," I thought as I watched myself reply. "He could have been really angry. But he wasn't."

On television, Lily was asking Danny her question. "Sir? Can you tell us why you think a car park is more important than a person's business?"

"He doesn't even look at her," Toby said. "I don't think Richmond's will be very happy with him."

"Listen!" Julie said, and I looked back at the television. A TV presenter was asking Lily Brookes questions now, and she was wearing my red dress. This was happening now.

"So, Lily," the presenter said, "you say this hairdresser cut your hair?"

The picture changed to a smiling Lily. "Yes, Simon," Lily said, "Sally Clarke cut my hair. And she gave me this whole new look."

The picture changed back to the presenter. "Well, I think you look great, Lily," he said, "really great."

The picture returned to Lily. "Thank you, Simon," she said.

"That was Lily Brookes reporting from the city center today," said the reporter when the picture changed back to him. "So," he said, "what do you think? Are big businesses like Richmond's the bad guys? Should we help small businesses to keep open? Give us a call or e-mail us at the usual address."

Toby was smiling. "Well done, Sally," he said. "You've really started something."

I was pleased, but a bit afraid as well. "I just hope I don't see Danny Dark anytime very soon," I said.

But of course, I did. The very next day.

Chapter 6

A date with Danny

I was just finishing drying someone's hair when he walked into the salon. My heart jumped, but I tried not to show how I felt.

"I won't keep you long," I told him, as if he were a customer. "Take a seat."

There's a small sofa in the salon for people who arrive early for their appointment. I keep some things for people to read on a small table next to it: newspapers and magazines about hair and fashion; gossip magazines too— magazines with stories about famous people and what they've been doing. Without saying anything, Danny sat down on the sofa and picked up one of the gossip magazines. The salon suddenly felt smaller with him in it, and the sofa looked like a toy. It wasn't just that he was a big man; it was . . . well, just him. He just seemed important, almost as if he were one of the famous people in the magazine he was looking at.

Yesterday I had been confident; yesterday had been a success. But today . . . well today I had a feeling I was about to pay for that success.

At last my customer's hair was finished, and he paid and left. Then I was alone with Danny.

"What can I do for you, Danny?" I asked, but he didn't look up from the magazine.

"Did you know that Lana Davis went to a big Hollywood party in a dress everybody could see through?" he asked, talking about what he'd read in the gossip magazine.

"Really?" I said.

"Yes," Danny said. "And Mimi Tucker went in a dress that was very short."

"What do you want, Danny?" I asked him angrily.

Finally, Danny put the magazine down, but he didn't get up from the sofa. Instead, he put his hands behind his head and looked up at me with a smile. "To see Mimi Tucker's dress?" he suggested.

I didn't think it was funny. "Well, try going to Hollywood," I suggested. "Mimi doesn't come to The Long and Short very often."

He smiled. "I'm sure she will soon," he said, "after such an excellent television story."

I looked at him anxiously. "You saw it then?"

"Oh yes," Danny said, "I saw it. So did my boss. He's not very happy."

I lifted my head. "I can't help that," I said.

"No," said Danny, surprising me. "It's not you he isn't pleased with; it's me. He can't believe I haven't dealt with this 'little problem,' as he calls it, yet."

I remembered what Danny had said the day before. Was his job really at risk?

"I'm sorry," I said. "It isn't personal, any of this. I'm just trying to save The Long and Short."

"I know that," Danny said, standing up. "And I'm just trying to buy it from you. There's nothing personal about that, either. I'm just doing my job."

"I know you are," I said, but actually every time I dealt with Danny it did feel personal. Every time we spoke or argued, it felt like a lot more than "just business."

"Look," he said. "Come out with me, Sally. Come out to dinner with me."

I was surprised. "Why?" I asked.

"Because it would be fun? Because it would . . . I don't know . . . make things right between us? I don't know, does there have to be a reason?"

"Yes," I said, "I think there does." It would be silly to accept his invitation. Really silly.

"OK," said Danny, "let me think. I know, it's 'World Say Yes to Danny Day.' How about that for a reason?"

I smiled. I couldn't help it.

Danny smiled back. "Please say you'll come, Sally."

I looked up. It was the wrong thing to do. Danny was looking down at me, and somehow I couldn't look away.

"Please," he said again in a soft voice that made me feel as if I were in a dream.

"All right then," I heard myself say.

Danny smiled again. "Great. Do you want me to pick you up from your home?"

"No," I said quickly. "I'll meet you back here."

He turned toward the door. "OK," he said, "I'll meet you back here at eight o'clock."

Next moment he was gone.

Danny's car stopped outside The Long and Short at exactly eight o'clock.

"Hello," I said nervously. "I wasn't sure what to wear. You didn't say where we were going, and I wasn't sure if it was going to rain or not . . ." I was speaking in a hurry, saying too much. I couldn't remember when I had last felt so anxious about a date. Nervous.

"You look lovely," Danny told me when I finally turned around.

"Do you think so?" I said doubtfully, looking down at the blue dress I had decided to wear, the sixth or seventh dress I had tried on. There were clothes all over my bed at home.

"Yes," Danny said. "And as it's 'World Say Yes to Danny Day' I've arranged for it not to rain this evening. So I suggest we walk if that's OK with you? The restaurant isn't far away."

Danny's joke about the rain made me feel more relaxed, and I began to walk beside him with a smile. "You can even control the weather then, can you?" I asked, and he smiled down at me.

"Of course. The weather does just what I tell it to do."

"Not like certain hairdressers?" I said, and this time he laughed.

"Yes," he agreed, "not like certain hairdressers. But let's not talk about that. I hope you like Mexican food?"

"I love it," I said.

"Good. I thought we'd go to Rosita's."

I stopped walking suddenly, making him stop, too. "That's great," I said. "But let me just say that if you think that by buying me dinner you can make me sell The Long and Short to you, you're wrong. It's not really 'World Say Yes to Danny Day.'"

He looked at me. "It was never in my thoughts," he said.

Rosita's was busy, but Danny had telephoned that afternoon, and we were shown to a nice table by the window.

"Shall I take your jacket?" Danny asked me.

"Thank you," I said, and as we sat down and I began to study the menu, I wondered how long we could continue to be so nice to each other.

I hadn't told either Julie or Toby I was coming here this evening. I didn't think I would be able to explain it to them. I couldn't really explain it to myself. Danny and I were at war with each other, and here we were about to eat a meal together. It didn't make a lot of sense if you thought about it too hard, so I decided I wouldn't.

After we had ordered, I looked at him across the table. Had I really only known him for a week? I couldn't believe that was all it was. So much had happened in such a short time. It was difficult to remember a time when I hadn't known Danny.

He was looking at me across the table. "What is going through your head?" he asked.

I looked down, playing with my knife and fork. "That's something else you can't control, I'm afraid," I told him. "My thoughts. Although actually, I was only thinking that I don't know much about you."

"What would you like to know?" he asked.

"What you think of me?" I thought. "Whether you find me as attractive as I find you?"

"I don't know," I said. "Your favorite color." It was all I could think of to say.

"Blue," he said, looking at my dress. "What's yours?"

"I haven't got one," I told him.

"You must have," he said. "Everyone's got a favorite color!"

"If I'm feeling happy, then it's usually red. But if I'm not, then . . ."

"Don't tell me," Danny said. "If you're unhappy, it's blue!"

"Well, yes," I said, "sometimes . . ."

"And she's wearing blue tonight!" Danny said, his hands to his face. "To think I thought everything was going to be OK!"

He was joking, and I laughed. "No," I said, "tonight this was the only dress that was washed and that fit. I've lost a few kilos lately." It was true; I had lost a few kilos, mostly in the last week, but I didn't say that.

"OK," Danny said. "My go. Your favorite place for a vacation."

"Greece," I said. "The Greek Islands. The sea is so beautiful. And yours?"

"Las Vegas."

I looked at him. "Really?"

"Sure!" he said. "It's fun, amazing, and the best way to get away from real life that I know."

"I'm surprised," I told him, and he smiled.

"I don't know why," he said. "You've seen what I'm like amongst fields and trees. I don't think the countryside suits me!"

"True," I said, playing with my knife and fork again. I loved the countryside so much, and I had an idea I would hate Las Vegas. Though I don't know why I cared. Danny and I were never going to get together anyway.

"You've gone away somewhere again," Danny told me, realizing I wasn't paying attention. "You do that a lot,

I've noticed."

"Doesn't everybody?" I asked, and he shook his head.

"Not my last girlfriend, you know, the one I moved to the UK for. She mostly just talked. She didn't think about things too much. When we broke up, I couldn't believe how quiet it was."

"It must have been hard," I said.

"Sure," said Danny. "That was mostly because I'd changed my life so much to be with her. It's not easy moving to a new country. Now I look back, I'm pleased we broke up. She wasn't the right one for me." He smiled, changing the subject. "OK, I've got the next one. Your worst break-up."

My face went pink. My worst break-up was a much deeper subject than what my favorite color was. "It was my turn to pick the subject next," I told him.

"You can have two turns after this," Danny told me. "Go on, your worst break-up."

I thought about it, although I don't know why, because I knew the answer right away. "My worst break-up was with my last boyfriend, Tony," I said at last. "I caught him in bed with a friend of mine."

"Oh," said Danny. "That's bad."

"It was bad, yes. But like you, now I'm pleased it happened. He wasn't a very nice guy."

"Wasn't he?"

"No. He was always telling me what to do; I didn't like that. And he made me feel bad about myself. It was a very unhappy time in my life." I looked up at Danny sadly. He was looking right back at me, and his face was so . . . kind,

I thought I might cry. "Look," I said, "do you think we could talk about something else?"

"Of course," he said softly. "But only after I've said how much I hate this Tony."

I continued looking at him, wanting to say, "But you're doing it, too. You're making me unhappy now, trying to take The Long and Short away from me." But I didn't, because I knew if I did, we'd start talking about it all, and that would be the end of the evening. And I didn't want the evening to end. Maybe this evening was my Las Vegas—my way of escaping from real life for a while.

It was a wonderful evening. Danny and I got on so well together. We talked, we ate, and we laughed a lot. But of course, eventually, the evening had to end.

After we'd left the restaurant, we stood outside, and Danny looked down at me.

"This was fun, wasn't it?" he said.

"Yes," I said. "It was a lot of fun."

"Then let's do it again," he said. "Soon."

I looked at his smiling face. While he still smiled like that, as if he and I were alone despite the other people walking past us along the street, then I could keep hold of the happiness of the evening. I could keep hold of my Las Vegas.

But I took too long to reply, and the look on his face changed. "But I still work for Richmond's, right?" he said. "So maybe that's not possible."

I could really care about Danny if this problem of Richmond's and The Long and Short didn't lie between us; I knew I could. He was impossible. He made me so angry sometimes. But he also made me laugh. And he made me want to touch him. He made me want him to touch me. Perhaps I already cared about him quite a lot.

But the problem of Richmond's and The Long and Short was between us. I couldn't just pretend that it wasn't.

"It might be difficult," I agreed quietly. "Tonight we've managed to forget about it all, but we wouldn't always be able to do that."

Danny's face was sad. "True," he said. "It's not fair, is it?"

"No," I said. "It's not."

He lifted his hand to touch my hair. "I'll drive you home," he said.

I didn't argue. We walked back to the salon and got into his car. The journey took less than five minutes. Five silent minutes during which I was aware of Danny's hands on the wheel as he drove and Danny's breath on my face when he looked at me.

"Turn right here," I told him, and soon we were outside my flat. I tried to smile, but I don't think it worked. "Thank you for a lovely evening," I said.

"That's OK. I enjoyed it too. Very much," he answered quietly.

"Good night." I got out of the car and closed the door. As I walked to my front door, Danny opened the car window. "Good night, Sally," he said. "Sleep well." And then he drove away.

Chapter 7

The big idea

Next morning, the jobs for the new Richmond's hair and beauty salon were advertised in the newspaper. And Mr. Morris came in to see me.

"I know there are still three days until I have to reply to Richmond's offer to buy my shop," he said, "but I thought you should know that nothing's changed for me. I still want to sell."

I looked at him unhappily. "OK," I said. "But you'll wait three more days to give them your answer, won't you?"

"Yes," Mr. Morris said. "I'll wait. Since you ask me to. But it won't make any difference, I'm afraid. I'm sorry, Sally. I really am."

After he'd gone, I stared sadly out of the salon window at the Richmond building. There had to be something I could do. Something to make a difference. There just had to be, because I knew I didn't earn enough to pay for the maintenance of the building on my own. It would be okay for a few months, but the building would need work before winter. Without Mr. Morris to help me pay for it, it would be impossible. I stood by the window for several minutes trying to think of something I could do. But I couldn't think of anything. Was this it? Was my fight to save The Long and Short really over? I turned from the window to look at my salon—the salon I had worked so hard to make a success. I really hated to think of closing. It was a very long morning.

At lunchtime, Julie came to see me. She brought me a sandwich, but I wasn't hungry. I showed her the job ads in the newspaper. "You should go for one of the beauty jobs at Richmond's," I told her.

"I can't do that," she said. "Don't be silly."

"Of course, you can," I said. "You hate working in that office. I don't expect you to give up your future because of me."

"I'm not giving up my future," she said, still refusing to look at the newspaper. "I don't want any job where somebody tells me what to do. I get enough of that at home, from Mum. 'Do the washing up, will you, Julie?' 'Clean the bath after you've used it, Julie.' I'm twenty-nine years old! I want to make my own decisions about when and how I do things!"

Was that the moment when I first began to get my big idea, I wonder? Or was it later on that afternoon, when two of my customers told me they still intended to use The Long and Short after Richmond's salon opened? I'm not sure, but when Lily Brookes came in just before I closed for the day, I was more than ready to hear what she had to say.

"Hi, Sally," she said. "I can't stop long. I just wanted to tell you we've had lots of calls to the TV station about our story on The Long and Short."

"Have you?" I said, surprised.

"Yes," Lily said. "Lots of women want to know whether you offer a makeover service, you know, new hair, new make-up, new clothes—a whole new look. It seems they really liked what you did with me. I thought I'd come and tell you about it. I thought you could do something with this."

I looked at her, feeling suddenly excited. "You mean, go into the makeover business myself?" I said.

Lily smiled. "Yes," she said. "I'd be happy to help, if you like. We could do another news story about you. Maybe have a competition as well, with the winner getting a complete makeover from you. We could show her before and after. When you've made her a new woman."

I felt excited and nervous all at the same time. "Do you really think it could work?" I asked her.

"Yes, I do," Lily said. "There's nothing like that in Norwich at the moment. Even the new salon at Richmond's won't be offering that kind of service."

I gave her a big smile. "It's certainly something to think about," I said.

"Well, let me know if you want my help. I'm happy to type something up to go with a business plan if you need me to."

"Thank you, Lily," I said, and she smiled.

"No problem. See you soon."

After she left, I just stood there for several minutes with excited thoughts going round and round in my head. It could work; it could really work. But it would be even better if I wasn't trying to do it all on my own.

After I closed the salon I went right to Julie's house. "Julie," I said as soon as she opened the door, "I've got a crazy plan that might just help both of us." And I told her all about it.

"We've both got money saved to buy our own flats." I spoke quickly, the words coming out in a hurry. "So I thought, if we put that money together, we might be able to buy Mr. Morris out. The newsagent's is big; there are lots of rooms behind the shop. I thought we could take down some walls and make one big salon—big enough to do hair, beauty, and clothes. And I thought we could both live upstairs, where The Long and Short is now. Of course we'd need to make some changes up there, but your dad's a builder; I wondered if he could help with that." I broke off to look at her. "What do you think?"

Julie had the biggest smile on her face. "I think it's a wonderful, wonderful idea, that's what I think!" she said. "I just don't know why I didn't think of it myself! Come on, let's go and talk to Dad now!"

So we went to speak to her dad, and he thought it was a good idea, too. The three of us sat talking about it for hours, and early the next morning before work, we all went to see Mr. Morris.

He was surprised to see us, but when I quickly told him about my idea, he was encouraging. "I'd be happy to sell the shop to you if you can raise the money, Sally," he said. "I couldn't sell for less money than Richmond's are offering though."

"If the girls can't raise enough money, I'll help them," Julie's dad told him, and Julie and I smiled at each other. "Do you mind if we look at the rooms at the back of the shop?"

"Not at all," Mr. Morris said, so we all went through the door to the rooms at the back of the shop to discuss how the rooms could be turned into a big salon. Then we went upstairs to The Long and Short to look at how that could be turned into a flat. It was all very exciting, and it was good that we had Julie's dad there to stop us from getting too excited. "You girls had better start work on your business plan and get an appointment with a few banks," he told us.

"Yes," I said. "You're right. I'll phone Lily Brookes now. Ask her to put her offer of running a TV story about the new salon in writing."

"And I'll call some banks and make some appointments," Julie said. "Come round again after work and we can start to type up a business plan."

It was a busy few days. There wasn't much time to think about anything else but the new makeover business. Though of course, I did still think about Danny. A little voice inside my head kept asking, "If I do this, if all this works out, will it change things for me and Danny? Will we be able to be together?" I didn't have any answers for myself. I just couldn't see things clearly anymore. I only knew I had to do this, because I couldn't lose everything. Not The Long and Short and a man I knew I could really care for. And if I gave up and didn't fight for my business to stay alive, I wouldn't be me. And I hoped it was the real me that Danny had begun to like.

Then, when Julie and I were sitting waiting anxiously at a bank for an appointment to talk about our business plan, my cell phone rang.

Julie was annoyed. "Sally!" she said. "Switch your phone off!"

But I had already seen that it was Danny. "I will, after this," I told her, answering the call.

"Hi, Sally," Danny said. He sounded . . . I don't know, a bit unhappy. Not like the Danny I was used to.

"Hello, Danny."

"I was thinking about you," he said. "I just wanted to know how you were."

Julie was looking at her watch. "Our appointment is in two minutes," she told me.

"I'm in the middle of something important actually, Danny," I said.

"Oh, OK," he said.

"Come and see me later," I told him quickly. "I might have some important news for you."

"I'm in London," he said. "I won't be back until late."

"Tomorrow then," I said. "Come and see me tomorrow."

He came at five o'clock the next day, just after my last customer had left. I recognized his step on the stairs.

"Hello," he said from the door, and my heart jumped at the sound of his voice.

"Hello." I had been putting used towels into a bag to take home to wash, but now I stood up to look at him.

He was smiling at me, but as he came closer, I saw that he looked tired. He looked different in another way too—he wasn't wearing his business suit; he was wearing jeans and a T-shirt.

"Haven't you been to work today?" I asked.

"No," he said, "I haven't."

He was standing really close to me now, and that electricity was at work again, moving all over my body.

"Day off?" I asked.

"In a way," he said. "I'll tell you about it in a minute. But first of all, tell me this big news of yours."

"OK." I felt anxious at first, as I began to tell him. But I was so excited about it all, it wasn't long until the words were hurrying out.

Then something about his smile made me stop. "You already know about this, don't you?" I guessed, and he laughed.

"Yes, I must admit, I do," he said.

"But how?"

"I phoned Mr. Morris yesterday, and he told me." He reached out to hold my hands, looking straight into my eyes. "Sally, it's great news," he said. "Well done!"

"You're not . . . you're not angry with me then?" I asked.

"Angry?" he said. "No! Not at all. I think it's wonderful. You must be so excited."

"I am excited," I told him. "But I must admit I'm a bit afraid, too. What if I fail? What if Julie and I don't get enough customers?"

"You won't fail," he told me. "It's a great idea. You're young, you're energetic, and you're going to be offering something different. I'm certain you'll succeed."

"I hope you're right," I said, and then I looked at him. "But what about you? Richmond's won't have their car park now."

"That's true," he said. "But as of today, that's their problem."

"What do you mean?" I asked, but I had already guessed.

"I mean I no longer work for them," Danny said.

I stared up at him. "You haven't . . . you haven't lost your job, have you?" I asked.

Danny's smile was dry. "Let's just say that Richmond's and I have agreed to say good-bye to each other," he said.

"You have lost your job," I said. "And all because of me. Oh, I'm sorry, Danny, I didn't want that to happen, I really didn't. But I just didn't want to lose my business, and . . ." I broke off, looking up at him worriedly.

"Of course, you didn't want to lose your business," Danny said. "I understand that; I've always understood that. Sadly, Richmond's didn't. When I told them they couldn't get the land for their car park, they were very angry. I decided I'd had enough, that I didn't want to work for a company like that anymore. So I told them I was leaving before they could tell me to leave."

I couldn't believe it. "But what are you going to do?" I asked him worriedly.

Danny smiled. "Me? I'm going to do the same as somebody I like and respect very much. Somebody who's about to become the owner of a highly successful new business."

By now I knew he was speaking about me, and my face went pink.

"I'm going to work for myself," Danny said. "There are lots of building projects out there that need experienced managers. I'll be all right. In fact, I'm excited about it."

But he didn't sound excited to me. I thought he was trying to be happy about it all, but really he sounded . . . well, a bit lost. "Are you sure?" I asked him.

He made a face then. "Well, OK, it's all a bit uncertain. I admit I'm a bit afraid about it all. I just hope I can find enough work. But I am excited, too."

"Really?" I asked, and he smiled.

"Really," he said. "It will be good to be doing something new. And I haven't been happy with the company for a while. It's not good to work for company you don't like."

I smiled back. "Well then, I'm happy for you," I said.

"Me, too," he said. "Good things will come out of this, I know they will."

"Yes," I said. "I think you're right."

"In fact," Danny said, "so much has happened so quickly. Do you realize it's less than two weeks since you first threw me out of here?"

"Well," I said, "I didn't exactly throw you out."

"OK," Danny corrected himself. "Since you told me to 'get

out.'" He gave a little laugh. "I was impressed, you know, I really was."

"Were you?"

"Yes," he said. "I could see I had a fight ahead of me. I liked that. I was just sorry that the fighting meant you wouldn't come out with me, because I wanted to ask you out on a date right away."

He was standing so close to me that by now our bodies were almost touching. The electricity was very strong, and it was an effort for me to speak. "I . . . I didn't know if you were asking me out because you liked me or as part of your plan to try to get The Long and Short."

Danny moved even closer. "Oh, because I liked you," he said, "always because I liked you. But I just didn't know how you felt about me. Until we went out for that meal. That meal gave me hope." He looked down at me. "Tell me, Sally," he said, "was I right to hope?"

I smiled up at him. "Oh, yes, Danny," I said. "You were right to hope."

He looked down at me and smiled. "Oh, good," he said, and then he kissed me.

It was a long time before either of us spoke again. Then at last Danny said, "Did I tell you I'm ordering a new sofa?"

I looked up at him and smiled. "No," I said, "you didn't."

"Well, I'm hoping you'll spend lots of time in my flat," he said. "And I don't think my life is going to be a white sofa kind of life any longer."

I remembered his white sofa and smiled. "What color is it going to be?" I asked him.

He smiled. "I don't know," he said. "But I can't wait to find out."

Review: Chapters 1–2

A. Match the characters in the story with their descriptions.

1. Sally Clarke
2. Danny Dark
3. Sam
4. Julie
5. Mr. Morris
6. Val

   a. manager of the builders

   b. Sally's best friend

   c. a customer at The Long and Short salon

   d. a newsagent

   e. manager of Richmond's building project

   f. owner of The Long and Short salon

B. Read each statement and circle whether it is true (T) or false (F).

1. Sally has her own business.   T / F

2. Sally is happy that a new store is being built next to her salon.   T / F

3. Sally is nervous when she meets Danny Dark.   T / F

4. Danny's ex-girlfriend lived in New York.   T / F

5. Danny offers to buy The Long and Short for £300,000.   T / F

6. Julie thinks Sally needs to be in a relationship.   T / F

C. Choose the best answer for each question.

1. Why do Sally's clients think she is "Sweet Sally"?

   a. She gives them candy.

   b. She's friendly to them.

   c. She's pretty.

2. How does Sally feel about Danny when she first meets him?

   a. She's attracted to him.

   b. She doesn't like him.

   c. She's angry with him.

3. How many staff does Sally employ?

   a. 1

   b. 2

   c. 0

4. Why does Mr. Morris want to accept Danny's offer?

   a. He wants to go on holiday.

   b. He thinks his business will fail.

   c. He needs the money when Richmond's opens.

Review: Chapters 3–4

A. Complete the crossword puzzle using the clues below.

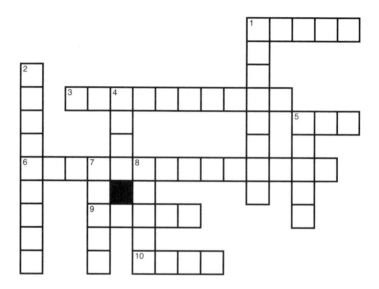

Across

1. a small bird

3. Sally's interview with Lily is shown on _____.

5. Danny falls down in the _____.

6. Sally goes running on _____.

9. Sally lends Lily a _____ to go with her dress.

10. Sally's brother

Down

1. Toby works as a _____.

2. The big store being built next door is called _____.

4. something you might use to a stranger in a bar: a pick-up _____

5. Sally has to put coins in a _____ to get electricity.

7. Danny's niece

8. a headline in the newspaper: Big Boots, No _____

B. **Read each statement and circle whether it is true (T) or false (F).**

1. Sally's shower is cold because she forgot to put the
   water heater on.   T / F

2. Danny loves the countryside.   T / F

3. Lily Brookes is a TV reporter.   T / F

4. Sally hopes the hair-cutting event will be on TV and in
   the newspapers.   T / F

5. Lily doesn't mind that her hair is wet.   T / F

6. Sally doesn't want to lend Lily a dress.   T / F

7. Lily is unhappy with how Sally does her hair.   T / F

C. **Choose the best answer for each question.**

1. Why is Sally excited when she buys a newspaper?
   a. She thinks she has won a prize.
   b. There is a story about her fight for The Long and Short in it.
   c. She is looking for a job, and it's Job Day in the newspaper.

2. Why does Sally like Mousehold Heath?
   a. It has good shops.
   b. You can get nice food to eat there.
   c. It's nice for walks or to go running.

3. What do we learn about Danny from the following conversation? "We
   have to take our shoes off in the hall!" Susan said. "And he doesn't let
   us eat pizza in front of the TV, until he's put a cover on the sofa,"
   Brian complained.
   a. Danny is very clean and tidy.
   b. Danny is a bad uncle.
   c. Danny is happy for the children to do what they like.

4. Why does Sally organize a big hair-cutting event?
   a. to meet up with her old friends
   b. so people will think she is clever
   c. to get on TV

Review: Chapters 5–7

A. Choose the best answer for each question.

1. A gossip magazine is . . .

   a. a magazine about hairstyles.

   b. a magazine with stories about famous people and what they do.

   c. a magazine of short stories.

2. Why does Danny say it is "World Say Yes to Danny Day"?

   a. It's his birthday.

   b. It is "World Say Yes to Danny Day."

   c. He wants Sally to agree to go on a date with him.

3. What is Sally's Big Idea?

   a. to start a makeover business with Julie

   b. to close The Long and Short

   c. to apply for a job at the new Richmond's salon

4. Why has Danny left his job?

   a. He has a new job.

   b. He's going to become self-employed.

   c. He's going back to America.

5. Why does Danny say he doesn't think his life will be a white sofa kind of life anymore?

   a. because Sally will spill coffee on the sofa

   b. because Danny doesn't like white anymore

   c. because he thinks life with Sally will be exciting

B. Fill in the blanks in the summary.

Danny goes to see Sally at the salon. He asks her out on a date. Sally says
1. _____. They go to a **2.** _____ restaurant. They play a game,
asking each other **3.** _____. They have fun and get to know each other
better. At the end of the date, they both want to see each other again, but
know that will be difficult with the **4.** _____ between them. Next
morning, Mr. Morris tells Sally he still wants to **5.** _____ the
newsagent's. Sally feels her fight is over and when Julie calls in, she
suggests Julie should **6.** _____ for one of the beauty jobs at
Richmond's. Then Lily Brookes calls. She suggests that Sally could start a
makeover business, giving women a whole new **7.** _____. Sally is
8. _____ by the idea. She asks Julie if she will go into **9.** _____
with her. Julie **10.** _____. The girls ask Mr Morris. if he will
11. _____ his shop to them. He says **12.** "_____," and the girls get
busy making plans and seeing banks. Danny comes to see Sally at the
salon. He tells her he has **13.** _____ up his job with Richmond's. He
didn't like their way of working. Sally tells him about her plans. He thinks
the idea is **14.** _____ and says he is going to become self-employed,
too. Danny and Sally talk about how they **15.** _____ about each other.
Now that Danny doesn't **16.** _____ for Richmond's, their problems
are over.

C. Match the first and last parts of each sentence.

1. Danny's boss isn't happy with Danny because

d. she's been worried about The Long and Short.

2. Sally has lost weight lately because

e. to tell her about her business idea.

3. Sally thinks she could really care about Danny

f. he doesn't know if he will be able to get enough work.

4. Sally goes to see Julie

g. he hasn't sorted out the problem of The Long and Short.

5. Danny is a bit worried about being self-employed because

h. if the problem of The Long and Short wasn't in the way.

Answer Key

Chapters 1–2

A: **1.** f; **2.** e; **3.** a; **4.** b; **5.** d; **6.** c

B: **1.** T; **2.** F; **3.** T; **4.** F; **5.** T; **6.** T

C: **1.** b; **2.** a; **3.** c; **4.** b

Chapters 3–4

A: **Across:** **1.** robin; **3.** television; **5.** mud; **6.** Mousehold Heath;
9. scarf; **10.** Toby
Down: **1.** reporter; **2.** Richmond's; **4.** line; **5.** meter;
7. Susan; **8.** heart

B: **1.** F; **2.** F; **3.** T; **4.** T; **5.** F; **6.** F; **7.** F

C: **1.** b; **2.** c; **3.** a; **4.** c

Chapters 5–7

A: **1.** b; **2.** c; **3.** a; **4.** b; **5.** c

B: **1.** yes; **2.** Mexican; **3.** questions; **4.** problems; **5.** sell; **6.** go;
7. look; **8.** excited; **9.** business; **10.** agrees; **11.** sell; **12.** yes;
13. given; **14.** great; **15.** feel; **16.** work

C: **1.** g; **2.** d; **3.** h; **4.** e; **5.** f

Background Reading:
Spotlight on... *New Businesses*

A. Read this information about the success rate of new businesses and answer the questions below.

The latest figures show that two-thirds of new businesses survive at least two years, and just under half survive at least four years. This is a big change from the previous long-held belief that one-half of businesses fail in the first year and 95 percent fail within five years.

1. Are the survival rates for young businesses what you would expect?

2. Why do you think the chances of a business surviving seem to have improved?

B. Read this information about why businesses succeed and answer the questions below.

1. You start your business for the right reasons—for example, you have found a gap in the market and you want to work very hard.

2. Good management—you have the skills you need, for example, to sell or to deal with people.

3. Enough capital—you have enough money to put into your business to get it going.

4. Location—your business is located in the right place for it to be successful.

5. Planning—you have a good business plan.

6. You don't try to do too much too quickly—new businesses can fail if you try to become too big too quickly.

7. You have a good website—these days, all new businesses need to have a website. Almost three-quarters of the people who live in the USA use the Internet.

1. Which reason for success do you think is the most important?
2. Can you think of any other reasons why a business might succeed?
3. What sort of person do you think makes a successful business person?

Glossary

beautician	(*n.*) a person who cuts hair, does makeup, etc.
car park	(*Br. Eng.*) (*n.*) a parking lot
competition	(*n.*) an organized event in which people try to do a specific activity better than everyone else
envelope	(*n.*) a rectangular paper cover for a letter
hairbrush	(*n.*) a brush used for taking care of the hair
hairdresser	(*n.*) a person who cuts and styles hair
lorry	(*Br. Eng.*) (*n.*) a vehicle larger than a car used to carry things; a truck (Am. Eng.)
mirror	(*n.*) glass to look at oneself in
newsagent	(*Br. Eng.*) (*n.*) a shop for newspapers, magazines, etc.
parking attendant	(*n.*) a person who looks after a car park
parking ticket	(*n.*) an official notice placed on a car parked illegally
path	(*n.*) a narrow way or trail for walking or cycling
project	(*n.*) a specific task, piece of work
roof	(*n.*) the top of a building
salon	(*n.*) a shop usually related to fashion or beauty
scissors	(*n.*) a handheld tool for cutting with two blades
shower	(*n.*) a place to wash your body under water
towel	(*n.*) a piece of cloth or paper used to dry something
vampire	(*n.*) a monster that drinks blood, e.g., Dracula